Divination

A Beginner's Guide to the Many Methods of Divination

Lauren Lingard

Table of Contents

Introduction 1

Chapter One: What is Divination? 2

Chapter Two: Astrology 7

Chapter Three: Tarot Cards 13

Chapter Four: Runes 23

Chapter Five: Pendulum Dowsing 31

Chapter Six: Scrying 35

Chapter Seven: Numerology 41

Chapter Eight: Tasseography 52

Final Words 57

Introduction

Human beings are hardwired to seek out and make sense of patterns in the world around us. In fact, it is this talent for pattern recognition that enables us to understand our environment, and which sets us apart, intellectually, from other creatures. For as long as humankind, as we know it, has existed, people have been using this innate pattern recognition to practice the art and science of divination; seeking insight on the past, present and future through the interpretation of natural and man-made phenomena.

Ancient Aztec scryers stared into polished obsidian mirrors seeking messages or visions. Around 500 BC, Greek philosopher Pythagoras laid out his system of numerology, divining meaning from the numbers of syllables in a person's birth name. In the 17th century, Europeans began seeking patterns in the dregs at the bottoms of their teacups. Perhaps even you, yourself, used a Ouija board with your school friends as a child. These are just a few of the many methods of divination used throughout history and across the world to help humans find answers to life's questions—big and small.

This book aims to peel back the shroud of mystery that surrounds the practice of divination and make divination accessible and understandable to you, the reader. In this book, you will learn about some of the most popular forms of divination used today: Their practice, their methods, their history, and their origins. You will even learn how you can try out some of these divination methods for yourself.

Whether you're relying on the wisdom of ancient runes to guide you through a difficult life decision or are merely curious about what your dreams have to tell you, the practice of divination can help you find answers—for those who are empowered to seek them.

Chapter One: What is Divination?

To *divine* (from the Latin *divinare*, "to predict") is to gain insight about the unknown through supernatural or occult means. The words divination and fortune-telling may be used interchangeably, though oftentimes the term divination implies more formal and ritualized methods. Outside its dictionary definition, the word divination connotes a relationship to divinity or godliness—but divination does not necessitate a deity or a blessed holy person to perform it.

This broad definition leaves room for dozens of types of divination practice, from the reading of animal entrails to the reading of playing cards. A divination practice can be related to a religion or spiritual practice; it can come from cultural or folklore practices. Seers, psychics, oracles, shamans, priests, and prophets can all be considered to practice divination, in one form or another, when they describe interpreting omens, seeing visions, or hearing the voice of God.

This definition of divination also leaves open to interpretation from whence the insight, inspiration, or knowledge is gleaned—from God or a divine being, from nature or a benevolent universe, or simply from the intuition of the diviner.

As you can see, "divination" is a very broad term that encompasses much and means different things to different people. To help us make sense of the wide world of divining, we can break down divination practices into types or categories. We will do this categorizing by asking three essential questions: *What* is being used to divine (the means), *how* is it being used by the diviner (the method), and *why* is it being divined (the motive)?

Means of Divination

Categorizing divination practices by *what* phenomenon is being interpreted (what is the material being used; the subject matter being observed?) is likely familiar to you. This is the conventional method for giving names to forms of divination. Examples range from the commonplace, to the bizarre and include:

- Aeromancy—divination by weather conditions
- Astrology (or astromancy)—divination by celestial bodies
- Cartomancy—divination by cards
- Felidiomancy—divination by cats
- Hydromancy—divination by water
- Lunomancy—divination by the moon
- Margaritomancy—divination by bouncing pearls
- Necromancy—divination by the dead or corpses
- Palmistry—divination by the lines on the human palm
- Scatomancy—divination by excrement

Since the possibilities of what, exactly, is being observed or interpreted are nearly endless—according to our broad definition of divination—an exhaustive list of the means of divination would be a long list, indeed!

Some of these means are grouped into broader named categories, but not all types of divination fit into these categories. These major groups include: Theriomancy, bibliomancy, scrying, cleromancy, and somatomancy.

Theriomancy, or zoomancy, is divination by the behavior and appearance of animals. This group includes augury or ornithomancy (divination by birds) and even ailuromancy or felidomancy (divination by cats).

Bibliomancy is divination by the written word or books and is typically (though not always) through sacred texts. Some sacred texts commonly used in bibliomancy include "The Bible" and "I Ching". Bibliomancy, as a category, also includes rhapsodomancy, or divination by poetry and song.

Scrying includes any form of divination that involves looking into, or staring into, a medium in hopes of gaining visions or other insight. This includes the use of crystal balls as well as hydromancy—scrying using a surface of water.

Cleromancy is one of the most varied and popular forms of divination. Cleromancy brings in the element of randomness or chance. Any method of divination that shuffles, scatters, or otherwise disrupts, and disorders the means before interpreting them is a type of cleromancy. For example, tarot cards and runes are typically shuffled and mixed before the diviner chooses a card or a token. Cleromancy also includes the practice of tasseography, or reading tea leaves.

Finally, **somatomancy** involves the reading of human body parts. This includes phrenology (divination by the shape and size of the head), palmistry, and the reading of various human bones.

We will revisit some of these means in later chapters when we explore the popular types of divination used today.

Methods of Divination

If we ask ourselves *how* the diviner is using the means of divination rather than *what* they are using, we can classify the method of divination. There are three categories of divination methods: Inductive divination, interpretive divination, and intuitive divination.

Inductive divination depends on the reading of natural phenomena with little or no manmade interference. Possibly the oldest form of divination, inductive divination often involves direct observation of the natural world, with meanings ascribed to various natural phenomena. One famous example of inductive divination is the Roman practice of augury, or divination from the behavior of birds.

Interpretive divination combines natural phenomena with some form of human manipulation, such as by casting stones. In interpretive divination, the diviner uses tools of some kind to interpret or focus the insight sought. This is as opposed to inductive divination, which does not manipulate its means. This is perhaps the most common type of divination seen today, as evidenced by the popularity of tarot cards and runes.

In **intuitive divination**, the diviner is him—or herself—the method or the conduit; no (or few) human tools are used, and natural phenomena are not observed. Instead, the divination is said to take place internally and intuitively in the "sixth sense" of the practitioner. Clairvoyants and psychics are often intuitive diviners. Traditionally, someone is said to have a gift, or innate talent, that enables them to perform intuitive divination, whereas inductive and interpretative divination methods can be learned.

Some divination practices are firmly rooted in one method or another, while others often employ a mixture of methods. For instance, a tarot card reading may seem to lie firmly in the interpretive divination camp, but the reader may also employ intuitive divination if clear insight comes to him or her during the reading.

Motives of Divination

The motives for performing divination are as myriad as the means of divination explored above, but most come down to one basic tenant:

The seeking of knowledge or insight. Motives of ancient diviners may have been grand in scope, as early occultists sought to divine the will of the gods. More commonly today, when performing divination, we are seeking answers to more mundane and ephemeral questions such as, "Will I find love?" or "Is this career move right for me?"

Chapter Two: Astrology

Astrology is divination by the movement and relative positions of celestial bodies, chiefly stars, or constellations. Astrology can tell us much about our nature as people through the interpretation of horoscopes. A horoscope is an astrological chart, of which your birth chart or natal chart is one. Horoscopes are typically created or diagramed by astrologers, though, in modern times, there are many websites that can quickly and easily create a unique natal chart tailored to you.

The History of Astrology

The ancient Mesopotamians were the first astrologers, identifying planets and naming constellations as early as 6,000 BC. This likely began as a way to track and predict patterns in nature, including rainfall and drought, which were essential to agriculture. Around 700 BC, the Babylonians of Mesopotamia produced the zodiac wheel we still use today, and the oldest horoscope dates back to about 400 BC.

When Alexander the Great conquered Babylon, it was the Greeks who then took up what the Babylonians had created and expounded upon it to create what we know as western astrology today. Western astrology is the astrological system upon which we will focus in this book; it takes its name and many of the attributes of the zodiac signs from Greek language and Greek myth.

In ancient Greece, astrology was considered a respected science on the same level as mathematics and philosophy, and this attitude continued after the fall of the Roman empire. Throughout Europe as late as the 17th century AD, astrology had a star spot among the respected studies of the day. Even universities in the Middle Ages had astrology professors. The development and growth of astrology at this time happened right alongside of—and benefited from the study of—astronomy.

The popularity and acceptance of astrology as a practice began to decline as the Church rose to power in Europe, villainizing astrology as heretic. Even famous Galileo himself was forced to renounce his belief in astrology in order to avoid an untimely death at the hands of an angry church. Then followed "The Age of Reason" in Europe, wherein anything supernatural fell out of style in favor of more rational pursuits.

Astrology experienced a resurgence in the early 20th century alongside a renewed interest in mysticism and spirituality in Europe and the Americas. Around 1920, newspapers began to publish the sort of horoscopes that we still read today, getting astrology into the popular culture. Admittedly, though, these tabloid horoscopes only focus on the sun sign, and therefore fail to give a thorough astrological prediction, which has caused astrology today to be considered, at large, fanciful, and entertaining, rather than the serious pursuit it once was. But, as you will learn in the following section, there is much more to the practice of astrological divination than just the sun signs.

The Twelve Signs

Twelve signs comprise the wheel of the Zodiac, each one based on a constellation with its own unique characteristics said to influence personality and fate. The sun is said to be in a given zodiac sign at a specific time, cycling through the twelve signs over the course of a year. The sign that the sun was in during the day of your birth is your sun sign, which is likely familiar to you. The list below gives the time periods for each sun sign:

- Aries: The Ram (March 21 - April 19)
- Taurus: The Bull (April 20 - May 20)
- Gemini: The Twins (May 21 - June 20)
- Cancer: The Crab (June 21 - July 22)
- Leo: The Lion (July 23 - August 22)
- Virgo: The Virgin (August 23 - September 22)
- Libra: The Scales (September 23 - October 22)
- Scorpio: The Scorpion (October 23 - November 21)
- Sagittarius: The Archer (November 22 - December 21)
- Capricorn: The Goat (December 22 - January 19)
- Aquarius: The Water Bearer (January 20 - February 18)
- Pisces: The Fish (February 19 - March 20)

Your sun sign is also sometimes called your star sign, or simply your zodiac sign. This last name is a misnomer. You actually have many different zodiac signs: One for each of the planets in our solar system, and then some!

The planets and other celestial bodies cycle through the twelve signs at different rates of speed. For example, Pluto orbits the sun very slowly and thus only moves through zodiac signs once every twelve to thirty-one years. But, because the moon circles around the earth in about twenty-eight days, the moon spends about two to two-and-a-half days in each zodiac sign each moon cycle.

For this reason, to determine your entire—correct—birth chart or natal chart, you will need to use not just your birth date, but also your time of birth. There are many free calculators available on the internet that will produce your full star chart, listing which sign each celestial body was in during the exact time of your birth. The possibilities are too many to list in this book!

It is important to know more than just your sun sign. The three most important signs in describing who you are as a person are your sun sign, moon sign, and rising sign. If you have ever felt like you don't quite relate to the familiar description of your sun sign, the answer may lie in examining your moon and rising signs in tandem with your sun sign—in order to find the nuance described that makes you, you.

Your **sun sign** describes your core identity. This is why it is sometimes considered to be the major zodiac sign. The sun is a very powerful celestial body that rules over some of your most important and basic personality traits. Your sun sign can also provide information on your path in life and what destiny you are suited for.

Your **moon sign** deals with your inner world of feelings and emotions. This is the more secretive, romantic side of you, and it explains how you relate emotionally to the other people in your life. This is a good sign to look to when trying to determine if you are romantically compatible with a potential match, since you surely want to be compatible when it comes to your feelings.

Your **rising sign**, also called your ascendant, is the sign that was rising on the eastern horizon at the time of your birth, and it cycles through the zodiac signs throughout each day. In contrast to your moon sign, your rising sign actually determines how you present yourself to others and how you conduct yourself outwardly. It is your "mask" you show the world.

So, to get a good picture of what astrology has to say about you as a person, you would want to look at your sun, moon, and rising signs and determine how each sign has a specific effect on you based on the celestial body moving through it—that is to say, a Leo sun means something different than does a Leo moon. In the following sections, we will explore, in more depth, what each sign represents. You can refer to the section below once you know your sun, moon, and rising signs to get a clearer picture of what your birth chart means.

Element and Mode

Each sign has its own distinct characteristics, including element and mode. The element and mode tell you a lot about a specific zodiac sign and also help us group zodiac signs together, which is helpful when we talk about compatibility. These characteristics also help give us a shorthand by which we can understand some basic qualities about a sign, without having to dig deep into each sign's description, as we will do in the next section.

The possible **elements** and their meanings are:

- Earth (Taurus, Virgo, Capricorn): stability, dependability, practicality, feminine/yin energy
- Air (Gemini, Libra, Aquarius): invention, creativity, communication, masculine/yang energy
- Fire (Aries, Leo, Sagittarius): passion, action, achievement, masculine/yang energy
- Water (Cancer, Scorpio, Pisces): emotions, sensitivity, mystery, feminine/yin energy

The **modes** and their meanings include:

- Cardinal (Aries, Cancer, Libra, Capricorn): active, ambitious, independent, hasty
- Fixed (Taurus, Leo, Scorpio, Aquarius): stable, focused, determined, stubborn
- Mutable (Gemini, Virgo, Sagittarius, Pisces): versatile, intuitive, adaptable, inconsistent

So, if we start to put the pieces together, we can begin to get a picture of what each sign might individually represent, just from learning these four elements and three modes. For example, we might expect Gemini, as a mutable air sign, to be skilled in communication but flighty.

Practicing Astrology Today

How can you bring the practice of astrology and all its benefits to your life today? Your first step is to get your birth chart. You can do this by hiring a professional astrologer or simply by using free natal chart tools found readily available through an internet search. To get your birth chart from one of these free online calculators, you will need to provide your date, time, and city of birth.

Once you have your birth chart, seek out either the guidance of a professional astrologer or do more research on your own to better understand what your birth chart means—how all the pieces of the puzzle come together to make you, you.

Once you know a little bit more about the signs, you can start to use this knowledge to better understand your relationships with others. Ask your friends and family what their signs are; or find out their birth times and calculate their own natal charts.

Chapter Three: Tarot Cards

Tarot cards, sometimes simply called tarot, are a form of cartomancy, or divination by cards. These mystical cards hold an incredible power to reveal profound truths to those who know how to read and intuit their messages.

Tarot cards are also a beautiful thing to behold, with gorgeous artwork on each individual card, sometimes even having gilded edges and being stored in luxurious silks. For this reason, tarot cards can be an expensive form of divination to practice. This is not the most readily accessible form of divination covered in this book, but it is quite worthwhile to those who invest in it.

Tarot cards may be one of the most quintessential means of divination today. You've likely seen them in movies and on television, if not in person. Oftentimes, we see a tarot card reader as a mysteriously cloaked gypsy woman or witch; but in reality, anyone can be a tarot card reader, even yourself! It does not require any special magical ability, just your own intuition and a little bit of study.

The History of Tarot

Tarot cards as we know them today evolved out of a regular deck of 56 playing cards, not dissimilar to the common pack of 52 playing cards used around the world today. These playing cards were numbered, came in suits like wands and coins, and included pages, knights, queens, and kings. In the 14th century, Italian artists added an additional 22 cards they called triumph, or trump, cards. These cards, unlike the other cards in the deck, were fully illustrated with unique designs. These trump cards would become the major arcana cards of the tarot.

But these first tarot decks were not, in fact, designed for purposes of divination. They were merely playing cards meant for parlor games and amusement. In the 16th, 17th, and 18th centuries, cartomancy slowly rose in popularity, and diviners began assigning specific meanings to each card in the deck. The first tarot deck created specifically for the purpose of divination was released in 1791 by a French occultist named Jean-Baptiste Alliette.

It wasn't until 1909, however, that modern tarot really came to be, thanks to the collaboration of British occultist Arthur Waite and artist Pamela Colman Smith. Both Waite and Smith were members of the Order of the Golden Dawn along with the famous Aleister Crowley. Smith designed what we call the Rider-Waite or Waite-Smith tarot deck, which was unique at the time for illustrating each and every card in the deck—not just the trump cards. It is Smith's unique illustrations that most tarot card designs are based on today.

The Minor Arcana

In the tarot, the minor arcana is the name given to those original 56 numbered suit cards. The four suits in a tarot deck are pentacles, cups, swords, and wands.

Pentacles, also called coins, are the suit representing the element of earth. These cards are typically about finances and material or earthly concerns. The suit of pentacles corresponds to the suit of diamonds in a regular playing card deck.

Cups are the suit representing the element of water. They are sometimes called chalices. These cards are about emotion and intuition, representing a very feminine energy. The suit of cups corresponds to the suit of hearts in a regular playing card deck.

Wands is the suit representing the element of fire. This fiery suit is all about action and initiative, very masculine energy as opposed to the suit of cups. The suit of wands corresponds to the suit of clubs in a regular playing card deck.

Finally, the suit of **swords** represents the element of air. This suit is about communication and invention, often dealing with the higher, mental self. The suit of swords corresponds to the suit of spades in a regular playing card deck.

The minor arcana is made up of numbered cards in each suit—from ace to ten—with the addition of page, knight, queen, and king cards. Each one of these numbers in the suits have a specific meaning, seen as part of a journey from 1 to 10, inspired by or related in part to numerological practices. Put simply, these meanings are:

1. (Ace) New beginnings, opportunity, fresh start, potential
2. Partnership, duality, balance
3. Growth, creativity, friendship
4. Structure, foundation, stability
5. Conflict, change, instability
6. Cooperation, harmony, communication
7. Knowledge, reflection, spirituality
8. Action, accomplishment, mastery
9. Fulfilment, attainment, come to fruition
10. Completion, end of a cycle, chance to begin again (start back at the ace)

The page, knight, queen, and king, together, are referred to as the **court cards**. These court cards are often, but not always, interpreted in a tarot reading to represent an individual or an aspect of the querent's personality, rather than a comment on a situation in the querent's life the way the other minor arcana cards are interpreted. Put simply, the court cards can be interpreted as follows:

- Page: A youthful and energetic figure, or a messenger of new opportunities
- Knight: Still youthful and very action-oriented, but more mature than a page, or a messenger of change and action
- Queen: A nurturing person, more mature and wise, or a messenger of creativity and ideas coming to fruition
- King: The most mature of the court cards, with vast experience under his belt, stable, solid, and highly capable, or a messenger of the completion of a project

Understanding what each of the court cards, suit numbers 1-10, and the suits themselves represent, allows a tarot reader to quickly and easily interpret each of the 56 minor arcana cards. For instance, since we know that the suit of cups represents emotions and intuition and that the number 9 represents fulfillment, we can begin to see a complete interpretation of the 9 of Cups card as representing emotional fulfillment. In another example, we know that the suit of wands represents action and energy and that the Kings of the tarot represent maturity, success, and completion; so, the King of Wands may signal an accomplished individual, like a successful businessman.

The Major Arcana

There are 22 cards in the major arcana, originally called the trump cards. They are numbered 0 through 21, and each of these numbers has an important meaning in numerology. The number 22 itself is considered sacred; it is the base number for the Kabbalah system of numerology that arose out of Hebrew mysticism.

When seen in a reading, these major arcana cards have a stronger influence on a querent's situation than do the minor arcana cards. That is, when a major arcana card shows up in a reading, the reader knows that this particular situation referenced will be a long term one: Negative cards will take longer to resolve, and positive cards will extend their divine energy for longer.

The meanings of these cards can be studied in great depth, and if you are interested in learning more about tarot, I have a book available on Amazon that is dedicated to the meanings of the cards, where you can find a lot more detailed information than what can fit in this book. For now, here is a short explanation of the meaning of each of the major arcana cards.

The Fool (0) is numbered 0 rather than 1 because 0 is the number of unlimited potential. It is not technically considered to be the first card in the deck, but rather a special card that exists outside of the numbering system. This card represents new beginnings. The fool can represent a person who is spontaneous and maybe a little bit reckless—a free spirit. The "journey" through the major arcana cards is sometimes considered to be the Fool's journey; hence the card is numbered 0 and therefore is thought to be always present throughout the sequence of the major arcana.

The Magician (I) represents power, both real and magical. This card is all about manifestation: The magician has all the tools needed before him to make your dreams come true. In a reading, this card is a sign to move forward with a new project or idea and to take action.

The High Priestess (II) is the card of the divine feminine and represents spiritual power, intuition, and sacred knowledge. She signifies enlightenment and spiritual wisdom. In a reading, this card is a sign to trust your intuition.

The Empress (III) represents fertility and abundance. The energy of this card is supremely feminine. The Empress is a nurturer and a creator; often this card is about literal motherhood, but it can also be about creative ability. In a reading, this card is a sign of prosperity.

The Emperor (IV) the masculine equivalent to the empress, is the father card of the tarot deck, representing masculinity, authority, and structure. The emperor is a powerful leader who commands respect. In a reading, this card can be a sign of a leadership role.

The Hierophant (V) also called the Pope in some tarot decks, represents spirituality. This card is the masculine counterpart to the High Priestess; but in contrast to the High Priestess, this card is more about the structure and dogma of religion. In a reading, this card can be a sign to follow the rules.

The Lovers (VI) is a happy card that represents not only romantic love but friendship and other types of relationships. This card is all about harmony, and communication is necessary for harmony in relationships. In a reading, this card can be a sign to communicate your true feelings openly and honestly with your loved ones.

The Chariot (VII) represents strength, determination, action, and willpower, as depicted by the warrior driving the chariot. In a reading, this card can be read as a sign of encouragement or a reminder to stay disciplined.

Strength (VIII) represents strength, like the Chariot card, but in this case, Strength speaks more to inner strength than the outer strength of the warrior. This card says you have the ability within you to overcome any obstacle. In a reading, this card can be a sign that you have inner strength that is fueling you.

The Hermit (IX) represents introspection. Building on the Strength card's inner strength, the Hermit goes deeper into the self to find inner guidance through soul searching. In a reading, this card can be a sign that you should take some time off from the world to reconnect with your inner self.

The Wheel of Fortune (X) is the card of destiny and change, representing the cycles of life. This card tells you to have faith that the universe will work everything out in its own time: Trust in what you cannot see. In a reading, this card can be a sign of good fortune to come.

Justice (XI) represents the law and, well, justice, or fairness and truth. This card is about cause and effect: You will be judged according to your deeds; you will reap what you have sown. In a reading, this card can be a sign that a legal matter will be dealt with, or it can mean that you need to stand by your own decisions.

The Hanged Man (XII) represents letting go. This card tells you that you need to rest and take a pause, or else the universe will force you to do so. In a reading, this card can mean that you should surrender to fate, take a break, and not keep pushing at this time.

Contrary to what you may think, **Death (XIII)** is not necessarily to be taken literally in the tarot. Rather than representing literal death, this card is all about change. Remember that each ending is actually a new beginning in disguise. Change may not be easy, but it can often be beneficial. In a reading, this card is a sign that change is coming your way, like it or not.

Temperance (XIV) represents balance and moderation. This card challenges you to see all sides of a situation and remain calm in the face of a challenge. In a reading, this card can be a sign that you need to return to order and balance if you are feeling out of sorts.

The Devil (XV) is a largely negative card that represents the darker aspects of the self, such as addiction. However, this card can also be interpreted to be about sex! In a reading, the Devil card may be a sign that you need to confront your inner demons.

The Tower (XVI), one of the most feared cards in the tarot deck, represents a very sudden change and complete upheaval. When this card appears in a reading, buckle up, because the situation is about to get rocky. In a reading, this card is a sign that something big is about to happen, usually not for good. On the bright side, the benefit of destruction is the chance to start fresh and rebuild.

The Star (XVII) represents renewal, following the destruction of the Tower, and is all about divine energy, hope, and faith. This card means that anything is possible. In a reading, the Star can be a sign to allow yourself to dream.

The Moon (XVIII) represents fear and illusion—your darker side. This card can mean that nothing is as it appears. In a reading, the Moon can be a sign that it's time to let go of your negative thought patterns: The fear is all in your mind.

The Sun (XIX) represents success and positivity. Like the warm rays of the sun, this card is positive and optimistic. The Sun gives you strength and reminds you of the radiant energy that lives within you. In a reading, the Sun card may be a sign that everything will work out just fine.

Judgment (XX) represents spiritual justice, unlike the Justice card, which is more about earthly matters. Judgment represents a spiritual awakening and likely signals that an important decision needs to be made. In a reading, the Judgment card can be a sign that you are nearing the end of a long and difficult journey.

And finally, the **World (XXI)** is the last card in the deck and as such represents completion and coming full circle. In a reading, this card can be a sign to look back and appreciate how far you have come and how much you have accomplished!

Tarot Card Spreads

Now that you have an understanding of what the 68 cards in the tarot deck mean, we can begin to look at how the cards are used in the act of divination. As tarot is a type of cleromancy as discussed earlier in Chapter 1, the deck of tarot cards are shuffled to introduce the element of random chance, and cards are then drawn either by the reader or the querent (reader's choice). These cards are then often laid out in a specific spread, where each card pulled from the deck represents a specific question or aspect of the querent's life.

Some practitioners of tarot believe that a card has a different, opposite meaning if it is drawn upside-down or "inverse." Additionally, if a card falls out of the tarot deck while the diviner is shuffling the deck, many practitioners will take this to mean that the card has some significance for the querent and incorporate this card into the reading.

There are many difficult possible tarot spreads, and you can even find many books dedicated to them! Advanced tarot practitioners may even invent their own spreads, or read cards in intuitively chosen order. As a beginner, it is best to start out with a simple spread, such as a popular three card spread for past, present, and future.

1. The first card drawn represents the past.
2. The second card drawn represents the present.
3. The third and final card drawn represents the future.

Practicing Tarot Today

As you have learned, anybody can practice interpretive divination through tarot cards with a little bit of study. So how do you get started?

The first thing you'll need is a deck of tarot cards. There are almost infinite options, these days, to choose from! As a beginner, it may be best to start out with the classic Rider-Waite deck or something similar, as this familiar imagery can help you to interpret the meanings of the cards. But you can choose whichever deck calls to you. Many practitioners even own more than one deck of tarot cards.

You may have heard a superstition that a person is not supposed to purchase their own deck of tarot cards, rather they are only to be received as a gift. Many in the modern occult community reject this superstitious idea as a form of gatekeeping and insist that you may buy your own tarot card deck.

It is also a good idea to purchase a blank notebook in which you can record your own readings. Each time you do a tarot reading, record the cards you drew and the spread in which you drew them, and note your interpretations of the cards as they apply to the query. Over time, as you take notes in your tarot journal, you will start to see, more and more, the meanings of the cards and their relationships in the spreads, helping you to depend less on that big book of card meanings.

Once you have 1) your deck of tarot cards, 2) your tarot journal, and 3) a source for spreads and card meanings—either a book or a website—you are ready to get started! Try this get-to-know-your-deck spread to start off. Draw 5 cards. These cards represent:

1. Your tarot deck's strength
2. Your tarot deck's weakness
3. What your tarot deck is here to teach you
4. What can you do to get the most out of your relationship with this tarot deck
5. What is the highest and best outcome of your relationship with this tarot deck

Chapter Four: Runes

The ancient symbols known as runes are in fact letters in the Runic alphabet, also known as Futhark. There is evidence that, in addition to serving as a regular alphabet, the ancient and medieval Norse peoples used runes for magic, called Runic Magic or Runecraft. In fact, the word rune comes from the Old Nurse word *rún* meaning "secret," strongly implying that there is more to runes than simply an alphabetic system. Runic Magic is still practiced today by pagans and occult practitioners as a form of divination.

Runic Magic today is typically practiced as a form of cleromancy, similar to Tarot Card readings: Runes are drawn at random, displayed in specific set ups or spreads, and interpreted based on their relative positions. Runes are typically cast using small rune stones or tiles on which a single rune symbol is carved. The runes are interpreted based on their ancient meanings and ties with Norse mythology. The diviner can find, in the runes, solace, insight, and even a glimpse into what is to come in the future.

The History of Runes

No one is really sure about the origins of the runic alphabet. Some speculate that it is based on an early version of the Greek alphabet, based on similarities between some of the letters, but this is not known for certain. The runic alphabet evolved, somewhat over time, leading to several different variations of the alphabet—including Older Futhark and Younger Futhark.

The earliest written incidence of Futhark, that is known, comes from the 1st century AD, but the majority of known writings in the Runic alphabet are from about the 11th century AD. Inscriptions in runes have been found across Europe, from Germany to the British Isles to Scandinavia. The Runic alphabet was the major alphabet used in Scandinavia throughout the Viking Age, until it was replaced by the Roman alphabet around 1200 AD.

While there is evidence that runic magic was practiced by the ancient Norsemen, we do not know many details about what their practice may have looked like. Instead, our modern use of runes for divination was developed and popularized in the 20th century.

The 24 Runes and Their Meanings

In a typical set of divinatory runes, there are 24 runes, based off of the Elder Futhark alphabet, and a single blank piece. This blank piece represents Odin's symbol, everything and nothing all at once, and is said to mean—in a reading—that the knowledge you seek cannot be revealed to you just yet.

The remaining 24 pieces are divided equally into three groups of 8. These three groups of runes are called **Freyr's Aett, Heimdall's Aett,** and **Haeg's Aett** (where *aett* means family).

The runes in Freyr's Aett are representative of the material plane and earthly concerns, including worldly possessions. Freyr in Norse mythology was a peaceful fertility god—son of Njörd, god of the sea. The eight runes in Freyr's Aett are:

1. ᚠ - **Fehu:** Fehu means cattle but is most often interpreted as signifying material wealth. This rune foretells abundance, luck, wealth, and hope. In a reading, fehu is a sign that a windfall of some kind is coming your way—be it a paycheck, an inheritance, or a less literal payout. If read in

reverse (called *merkstave*), fehu can indicate a coming financial loss or a loss of personal possessions.

2. ᚢ **- Uruz:** Uruz means ox or wild bull, representing supreme strength and endurance. This rune has a very masculine energy. In a reading, uruz can be a sign that your power is increasing, or that you are experiencing a period of great energy and accomplishment. In the reverse, uruz might indicate a lack of endurance or being dominated by others.

3. ᚦ **- Thurisaz**: Thurisaz represents Thor's hammer or, alternatively, a giant. This rune signifies a powerful force of energy, either positive or negative—either used as a destructive weapon or used defensively. Thus, thurisaz often represents a challenge or danger in a reading. Reversed, thurisaz could mean that you are feeling defenseless in the face of life.

4. ᚨ **- Ansuz:** Ansuz means "message" and is closely tied to Odin the Allfather. This rune represents communication, often indicating in a reading that a message will be coming—perhaps even a divine message. Ansuz can also be interpreted as truth, or wise, good advice. Reversed, ansuz signifies bad communication: misunderstandings or deceit.

5. ᚱ **- Raidho:** Raidho means journey and is signified by a wheel. The journey represented by raidho could be literal travel or a spiritual adventure; either way, in a reading, this rune typically indicates progress of some kind. This rune can also be read as a sign of the cycle of life. Read in the reverse, raidho could mean stagnation or rigidity.

6. ᚲ **- Kenaz:** Kenaz means flame or torch. The flame of kenaz is the beacon of truth, representing enlightenment and knowledge. In a reading, kenaz may be a sign of secrets

revealed: something previously unknown to you will soon come to light. Kenaz can also indicate inspiration and creativity. In the reverse, kenaz might represent a lack of vision or a creative block.

7. **X - Gebo:** Gebo means gift. This is a happy sign, one of joy and generosity. In a reading, gebo may indicate that you will soon be blessed with a bounteous gift. This rune can also mean that you already have the gifts and talents you need to succeed. Gebo is not read in reverse because the X-shaped rune is read the same regardless of its orientation.

8. **ᛈ - Wunjo:** Wunjo means "joy." This is a symbol of peace, happiness, comfort, and pleasure, signifying the clan's victory flag. In a reading, wunjo can be a sign that triumph is on the horizon for you. You will reap the rewards and live in comfort. Reversed, wunjo may indicate sorrow, loss, and being alone.

The runes in Heimdall's Aett represent growth and a journey into maturity. These runes tell us about obstacles we will face and what our fate will be. In Norse mythology, Heimdall was the watchman of the gods. The runes in Heimdall's Aett are:

9. **H - Hagalaz:** Hagalaz means hail or hailstorm and, like the natural force to which this rune refers, it signals a cataclysmic change, much like The Tower card in the tarot deck. When hagalaz appears in a reading, it often signifies a great trial that the querent must weather gracefully—a test, if you will. This rune is not read in the reverse, for it has no reverse.

10. ↑ - **Nauthiz:** Nauthiz represents your needs as a person. When this rune appears in a reading, it may be a sign to consider whether you have enough balance in your life—are your needs fulfilled in all areas? Nauthiz can also point to a delay or some type of restriction. Nauthiz has no reversed meaning because it cannot be read in the reverse.

11. **I - Isa:** Isa means "ice," in this case, representing a pause or break—as if the querent were stuck frozen in a sheet of ice. Isa may indicate frustration with the feeling of being stagnant or stuck, but take it as an indication to take a "chill pill" and enjoy the stillness. Isa cannot be read in reverse and therefore has no reversed meaning.

12. ♦ - **Jera:** Jera represents the harvest and in a reading suggests that you may reap what you have sown—abundance will follow! If you draw this rune when you are feeling like you don't have much in the way of blessings, take jera as a sign to stop and practice gratitude for what you do have. Jera also represents mother nature and the cycle of the year. It has no reversed meaning.

13. ↕ - **Eihwaz:** Eihwaz means yew tree, which in Norse mythology is closely tied with Yggradisil, or the Tree of Life. Eihwaz is therefore representative of sacred knowledge. This rune can be compared to the Death card of the tarot, as it represents the turning of the cycle of life. Eihwaz does not have a reversed meaning.

14. ⌐ - **Perthro:** Perthro translates to "destiny" and is closely tied to fortune; therefore, it is sometimes called the gambler's rune, representing the cup of dice. In a reading, perthro is a sign that you are not in control of your fate, that

you need to learn to roll with the punches, as it were. In the reverse, perthro may be interpreted as loss of faith.

15. **Y - Algiz:** Algiz means elk, representing protection as a large beast with powerful antlers. This rune essentially acts like a spiritual shield guarding one against evil forces. Algiz can also indicate in a reading that a spiritual transformation is on its way. Reversed, this rune indicates that a hidden danger awaits you.

16. **ᛋ - Sowilo:** Sowilo is the sun, representing joy, abundance, warmth, good luck, and success. When you see this rune in a reading, take it as a call to celebrate your accomplishments. You are entering a peaceful and joyful period. This rune cannot be read upside-down and so has no reversed meaning.

The final set of runes, Tyr's Aett, is named for the god of the sky, Tyr, who represented justice and war. The runes in Tyr's Aett speak to our lasting legacy and our developed spirituality. They are as follows:

17. **↑ - Tiwaz:** Tiwaz is the arrowhead, closely tied to the god Tyr. This is a symbol of victory. In a reading, tiwaz indicates that you are spearheading whatever troubles life throws at you. Tiwaz has great leadership energy. Read in the reverse, tiwaz may indicate a lack of passion or an imbalance in the heart and mind.

18. **ᛒ - Berkana**: Berkana means "birch tree." This rune represents birth, both literal and figurative, and is closely tied to the Birch goddess of Norse myth. In a reading,

berkana may indicate renewal or new beginnings. Read in the reverse, berkana represents trouble within the family.

19. **ᛖ - Ehwaz:** Ehwaz is the horse. This rune represents moving forward, as in the time of the Vikings, horses were the major means of travel by land. In a reading, ehwaz indicates steady progress and a change for the better. This rune also represents harmony, as is found between a man and his horse. In the reverse, ehwaz can mean disharmony and mistrust as well as restless energy.

20. **ᛗ - Mannaz:** Mannaz means "man" and represents humanity and humankind as a whole. This rune is all about community and cooperation with the expected social order. In a reading, take mannaz as a sign to strengthen your relationships with others. Read reversed, mannaz can indicate isolation.

21. **ᛚ - Laguz:** Laguz means "lake" or "sea" and so represents the element of water: This rune is all about emotions and intuition. Like whatever lurks at the bottom of the water, laguz can be interpreted to contain unknown mysteries. In a reading, this rune represents an awakening of psychic ability. Read in the reverse, laguz might indicate a lack of creativity, as if the well has all dried up.

22. **ᛝ - Ingwaz:** Ingwaz is fertility and is closely tied to the god of Earth in Norse myth, Ing. In a reading, this card may indicate a pregnancy, but it can also point toward wellbeing, strength, and the family life. Ingwaz is a symbol of great virtue. This rune cannot be read in the reverse.

23. **ᛟ - Othala:** Othala means heritage and inheritance, but it is not strictly a material inheritance, rather a spiritual one. In a reading, othala may signify an alignment of your values

with what is truly important in life. Read in the reverse, this rune may be about negative karma.

24. **ᛞ - Dagaz:** Dagaz is the final run in the set, representing the dawn. At once, dagaz means an ending and a new beginning, representing a transformative change. In a reading, dagaz may be a sign that breakthroughs are on the horizon; it signifies hope and clarity of mind and spirit. This final rune cannot be read upside-down.

Practicing Runic Magic Today

Now that you know the meaning of each rune, you have the foundational knowledge required to perform a rune reading. All you are missing is the runes themselves, so it's time to get yourself a set!

Rune tokens come in many different materials and are sold at many different price points. Some of these materials are said to represent different energies and correspondences, so you may want to think carefully about whether bone, oak, or crystal runes are right for you. If you cannot find runes for sale locally, you may have better luck shopping online, where you are sure to find many options.

Once you have your bag of runes in hand, you are ready to begin. As a beginner, one easy way to practice reading runes is to pull one rune for yourself every morning to tell you about your day. There are also more complex rune spreads, similar to tarot card spreads. I have a book dedicated to the topic of Runes, also available on Amazon if you wish to learn about Runes in more depth!

Chapter Five: Pendulum Dowsing

Dowsing refers broadly to the divinatory practice of using an item that "points" in one direction to divine answers, most commonly the location of something. This is most commonly done with the use of a dowsing rod, sometimes called a divining rod, or using a pendulum. The basic premise of rod dowsing is that energy emitted from the object being sought out causes the rod to shake and move, and the dowser interprets these movements as indications of where to go until the object is found.

Today, the practice of dowsing can refer to two popular extant practices in the west: water dowsing—which commonly uses a rod to find groundwater or other underground objects of interest—and pendulum dowsing—which has expanded to include the use of pendulums over Ouija board-like grid charts in order to divine answers to queries. In this book, we will focus on pendulum dowsing, as it is the most popular form of divinatory dowsing in the western world today.

It is worth noting, however, that water dowsing is still practiced today to find the appropriate location to dig a well!

The History of Dowsing

This divination practice came into popularity in Europe during the Middle Ages, most likely as a means to locate precious metals within the earth. The earliest written record of dowsing as a practice dates to the 16th century in Germany mining villages. Though, there are some claims that images that appear to look like dowsing rods have been found in Egyptian art and carved on cave walls—implying that the practice is much older.

Eventually the church suppressed dowsing as an evil, occult practice, but peasants still had a need to find water and other materials underground. This may actually be why a forked stick came to be used some commonly for dowsing, as it could be gathered in secret and disposed of after use. During this time, dowsing with a pendulum also became popular among diviners. During the Spanish Inquisition, practitioners of pendulum dowsing were burned at the stake as witches and heretics.

By the 18th century, dowsers favored pendulums over dowsing rods in common practice, and the common use of dowsing shifted from searching for buried treasure to metaphysical purposes. Around the 19th century, interest in this divinatory art began to decline as the age of science and reason took over. But not all scientists of the time disavowed dowsing; the great Albert Einstein himself is said to have been a practitioner of dowsing, and he believed that science would one day have an explanation for the mechanism behind dowsing's effectiveness.

The new age movement in the west in the 20th century brought dowsing back into the public eye. Pagans and practitioners of the occult latched onto the art of pendulum dowsing as a simple, and accessible, method of divination and one that is especially adept at answering a quick yes-or-no question.

Practicing Pendulum Dowsing Today

Pendulum dowsing is easily accessible, both because it requires few tools and because it is believed by dowsers that dowsing is an innate human ability that anyone can do. You do not have to be a psychic to practice dowsing; dowsers believe that everyone has the capacity to sense and react to incoming energy through a pendulum or divining rod.

All you need to get started is a pendulum! Pendulums are most commonly made from a pointed crystal hung on a chain, but this needn't be a fancy crystal or even a crystal at all. You can use any weighted object on a chain that has a clear point to it. Pendulums are readily available for purchase at metaphysical shops or on the internet.

It is important that your pendulum feels "correct" in your hands. The pendulum is the conduit between you as the dowser and the psychic energy of the universe; it simply will not work if you do not feel the connection to your pendulum powerfully. You may wish to energetically cleanse your new pendulum using sage or palo santo smoke or some other type of cleansing ritual; or to sleep with the pendulum under your pillow to allow yourself to better connect with the new tool.

Once you have your pendulum, the actual process of dowsing is, in fact, quite simple. You may wish to test out the movement of your pendulum before you proceed to actually ask a question. The first thing you will want to do is make sure that there is no breeze in the room or any other factor that could affect the movement of the pendulum; ensure, for instance, that you are seated in a comfortable way that allows you to keep your hand perfectly still.

Now, hold the pendulum out with your dominant hand and keep quite still. Focus on the question you have to answer. After a time, you should begin to see the pendulum swing in some direction. What does this mean? Typically, a clockwise rotation means yes, while a counterclockwise rotation means no—but you should use your own intuition to interpret the movements of your pendulum, as this magic is unique to you and your instrument.

Once you have gotten the hang of answering yes/no questions, try incorporating an answer key grid into your practice for more advanced pendulum dowsing. These charts can be found online, or you can feel free to make your own. Simply use the pendulum as before, but watch to see which letter or phrase is indicated by the motion of the pendulum, much as you would with the movement of the planchette on the Ouija board.

Chapter Six: Scrying

The word *scrying* may not sound familiar to you, but you are likely familiar with its practice. The most famous example of scrying divination is the crystal ball, often used by psychics and seers in movies and books to tell the future. To scry means to gaze intently into a surface or object of some kind and interpret any visions you may see within. The word scry comes from the Old English *descry*, which means to discern or ascertain. Scrying is also sometimes called seeing or peeping.

There are many types of scrying, though, and you need not use a crystal ball to try it out for yourself. Any reflective surface, in truth, can be used for scrying. Some diviners even scry into a dark room or into a cloud of smoke! We will cover several examples in this chapter and even include a step-by-step guide at the end that you can try out with objects you probably already have on hand!

The History of Scrying

Scrying is perhaps one of the most ancient methods of divination still in use today. Many ancient cultures practiced a form of scrying independently of one another.

The Aztecs of Mesoamerica are perhaps the most famous of the ancient scryers. The Aztecs are known for their use of polished obsidian, a black mineral composed of volcanic glass, to scry with. Obsidian was considered sacred to the Aztec god of the sky, Tezcatlipoca. The ancient Greeks and Celts both practiced scrying as well, using beryl and other crystals.

Ancient Egyptians used water, oil, and mirror scrying in their rituals. In Egyptian mythology, it is said that the goddess Hathor possessed a special, magical shield that was capable of reflecting back the truth of all things. Hathor is said to have fashioned the first scrying mirror out of her magic shield.

The earliest written recording of scrying dates back to ancient Persia, where the practice is mentioned in the 10th century Persian text called the Shahnameh. This epic text describes what is called the Cup of Jamshid, which was used by wizards in pre-Islamic Persia to see all seven layers of the universe.

Even the famous seer Nostradamus, whose predictions are well known throughout the world today, is said to have scryed using a bowl of water! Later in this chapter, you will find a complete step-by-step guide to water scrying—like Nostradamus.

Despite being such a widespread practice in the ancient world, scrying—like most forms of ancient divinatory wisdom—was repressed by the church throughout the dark ages in Europe. It was not until the 16th century or so that scrying came into fashion again in the western world, when a scryer by the name Dr. John Dee reached fame.

Dr. John Dee was a famous alchemist, mathematician, and astronomer who served as an advisor to Queen Elizabeth I on matters pertaining to science and astrology. For this, Dee is known as the last magician to serve the British royal family. Dee was a serious, and well learned, academic who was also fascinated by the occult—especially divination. He spent his later years experimenting with different scrying methods in the attempt to communicate with angels.

Beginning in 1583, Dee joined forces with Edward Kelly and the pair began using the combination of a black obsidian mirror (like the Aztecs you learned about above) and a small clear quartz crystal ball for their scrying. It is said that Dee was successful in communicating with angels, who pointed out letters on a Ouija board-like grid that he had created.

Dr. John Dee and Edward Kelly paved the way for modern occultists and diviners, popularizing this ancient practice.

Popular Scrying Mediums

As mentioned earlier, practically anything can be used to scry as long as you can focus your vision on it. Here we will cover a few of the most popular scrying mediums used today. Many of these are readily available materials, meaning that these types of scrying are available to you without having to purchase any special equipment.

With any one of these mediums, the goal is to stare into them and go into a sort of trance-like state, relaxing your vision and clearing your mind. Eventually, images or phrases or visions should appear to you on the surface of your medium, but it may take some time staring to reach this state.

Crystal scrying, also called crystal gazing or crystallomancy, is the quintessential means of scrying, but you needn't use a crystal ball for it to count. You can use any crystal, such as a common quartz point or any stone with a reflective surface that calls to you.

Mirror scrying is one of the most common and oldest forms of scrying. It has its own name: Catoptromancy. All you need to do mirror scrying is a mirror or another highly reflective surface (like the polished obsidian used by the ancient scryers). You may choose to practice mirror scrying in dim lighting to better help you focus.

Water scrying, also called hydromancy, involves staring into water. This is either done with still water and a light source, staring as the reflections dance across the water's surface; or it's done less commonly with running water, such as scrying into a bubbling stream. The diviner may also drop objects into a vessel of water, such as pebbles, and interpret the patterns in the ripples that emerge.

Wax scrying, sometimes called carromancy, also utilizes water; in this case, melted wax (such as candle wax) is poured or dripped into a vessel of water, and the scryer stares at the wax to interpret the shapes it forms as it cools and solidifies in the water.

Oil scrying is similar to water scrying, only instead of the surface of water, the diviner scrys into a surface of oil. This can be oil in a vessel or oil poured onto a surface, even the body. The key here is in the light that is reflected off the surface of the oil.

Fire scrying involves staring into a flame and interpreting the images found there. This ancient method of divination can be done with a flame as small as a tealight candle or as large as a blazing bonfire. Related to fire scrying is **smoke scrying**, which involves the interpretation of images seen when staring into a fire's smoke.

Cloud scrying or cloud gazing requires the diviner to look up to the sky, where images can be seen among the clouds, be they dark and stormy or fluffy and white.

Practicing Scrying Today

As you've learned, there are many mediums used for scrying. Most of them you can come by easily, as you probably already have water, oil, mirrors, and more in your home.

If you would like to give scrying a try, try this water scrying ritual.

You will need:

- A shallow bowl (dark colored is best)
- Water (preferably fresh rainwater, but any water will do)
- A candle (or more than one) and something to light it with (matches or lighter)
- A crystal or another small object to act as a focus

Follow this step-by-step guide:

1. To begin, fill your bowl or vessel with water almost to the top. The reflective surface of the water in the bowl will act as the medium into which you will scry.

2. Next, drop a crystal in the bowl, making sure it sits right in the center of the bowl. You can use a basic quartz crystal or any other type of stone that calls to you. It does not have to be a crystal, per se, either; you can use any small trinket that is meaningful to you. The purpose of the crystal or trinket is to serve as a visual anchor for you to focus on while scrying.

3. Set your bowl up on a stable, flat surface in a quiet room. It may be best to set the bowl on a low table, so that you may sit on the floor in front of the bowl and have the scrying medium at your eye level. Set up your candle or multiple candles around and very near the bowl of water and light it/them. Turn the lights off in the room so that your candle(s) is/are the only source of light.

4. To set the stage, you may wish to turn on some instrumental music and light some incense. You may also like to burn some sage leaves or palo santo wood to spiritually and energetically cleanse the space before you get started. You can do anything you'd like to prepare your space, as long as your intention is to create a space that is peaceful and quiet; you want this space to foster your intuition.

5. Get comfortably seated, and when you're ready, begin to meditate and focus on your breathing (or another sound you can hear, like the music you played) until you enter a trance-like state. Your goal here is to reach an altered state of consciousness, and you will know you have reached it when you begin to feel strangely alert and expanded. This may

take some time, so remain patient. If you struggle to reach a trance-like state, try switching up your environment by playing different music (as one example).

6. Once you have found this altered state of consciousness, turn your attention to the bowl of water in front of you and begin to stare into it. Begin by focusing on the crystal or other object in the center of the bowl, then let your vision and the rest of your face relax. In your mind, focus on your intention for this scrying session: What is it you want to know? What answers do you seek? It is okay to let your mind wander, but try to keep your vision focused on that single point. After some time, you should begin to see visions in the bowl of water as the candlelight dances off of the surface.

7. Your scrying session is complete when you feel that you have received all the insight you will receive from the medium. When you feel you are finished, stand up slowly and turn the lights back on in your room. It is a good idea to ruminate on the experience and what visions or words came to you. You may want to start keeping notes on your scrying sessions in a journal so that you can refer back to this wisdom later.

It may take a long time of staring into the water for any clairvoyant messages to come to you, and it may not happen at all the first time you try scrying. Do not be discouraged. Just have patience and try again.

Water scrying may not work for you at all. If you do not feel drawn to this medium, feel free to explore any of the other types of scrying listed above until you find the type that works best for you!

Chapter Seven: Numerology

Numerology is an ancient system of divination based on numbers. Numerology is to numbers as astrology is to stars. Like the signs of the Zodiac, numbers—the most basic building blocks of the universe—influence us all profoundly from the time of our birth. Numerologists believe that understanding how we relate to these numbers and harnessing their power can help us to better ourselves and the world around us.

Numerologists use numerology charts much like astrologists create astrological, or birth, charts. These charts contain much wisdom and insight about an individual calculated by that person's full name and date of birth. A numerology chart includes multiple numbers that are calculated in different ways to provide different types of guidance and answers.

Types of Numerology

There are three major types of numerology, each one having originated in a different part of the world. No one type of numerology is better than the others, and they can actually be used together in a numerology reading—though this is not recommended for beginners, as mixing the different systems can get confusing.

The three major types of numerology are Kabbalah numerology, Chaldean numerology, and Pythagorean numerology.

Kabbalah numerology has its origins in Hebrew mysticism. This system of numerology is based on the sacred number of 22, which is also the number of Major Arcana cards in the Tarot. Kabbalah numerology places a great focus on letters and is thus most often used to divine meaning from birth names.

Chaldean numerology originated in ancient Mesopotamia. This is also where astrology originated, and Chaldean numerology has close ties to astrology. In Chaldean numerology, the single digit numbers 1-8 have unique vibrations, and each letter in the alphabet is assigned to one. The number 9, however, is kept sacred and separate in Chaldean numerology.

Pythagorean numerology is the most common type of numerology seen in the western world today and therefore, it is the system of numerology we will focus on in this chapter. Pythagoras, the Greek philosopher and mathematician, is credited with inventing this numerological system in the 6th century BC. Pythagorean numerology, like Chaldean numerology, says that each single digit number has a unique vibration. However, in Pythagorean numerology, all single digit numbers 1-9 are used. Pythagorean numerology, as we will see in depth later in this book, also venerates certain double-digit numbers, including 11, 22, and 33.

The History of Numerology

Numerology is perhaps one of the oldest forms of divination still commonly practiced today. Like astrology, numerology originated with the ancient Mesopotamians. It was the ancient Sumerians as far back as 3200 BC who first developed the numerical system on which later Mesopotamian mathematics and numerology were based. This original form of numerology is called Chaldean numerology, after the Chaldean empire.

When Alexander the Great conquered Persia, he brought back to Egypt with him knowledge and teachings of the ancient Babylonians—including numerological concepts. It was there in Egypt that Pythagoras, known as the father of western numerology, began his studies.

Pythagoras, a well-respected Greek philosopher and mathematician, built upon and expanded the Chaldean numerology principles to create the most popular form of numerology today. But the church repressed numerology, astrology, and other forms of divination throughout the dark ages, and it was not until the late 19th and early 20th centuries that numerology began to come back into fashion.

It is Mrs. L. Dow Balliett who is credited with first bringing Pythagoras's theories together with Christian numerological influences to create the beginnings of the western numerological system we know today. Balliett did so around the start of the 20th century. Her student, Juno Jordan, continued her work, going on to publish a book called "The Romance in Your Name" in 1965. The new age movement in the 1970s and onward helped propel the popularity of Jordan's work. This book first laid out many of the numerological calculations still used today. Other authors have since taken up the subject and built upon it, but Balliet and Jordan were truly the first modern day numerologists.

The Meanings of Numbers

In Pythagorean or western numerology, which is the type of numerology we will focus on in this chapter, each number 1-9 is said to have an innate cosmic meaning that includes personality traits, both positive and negative. The reason numerology deals primarily with single digit numbers, is because Pythagoras believed that these numbers were the building blocks of the universe. As such, all double-digit numbers can be broken down into a single digit number by the sum of their digits. Numerologists call these numbers **Root Numbers**. An abbreviated explanation of the meanings of each single digit number are below:

1. The **Number 1** in numerology, the first number, represents new beginnings, opportunities, and momentum. Spiritually,

the number 1 represents the very birth of the divine universe.

2. The **Number 2** in numerology represents partnership and harmony. It is considered a very feminine number. The number 2 serves as a mediator and peacemaker, bringing balance with it.

3. The **Number 3** in numerology represents creative expression and communication. It is a number that dances through life, a social butterfly, and a very creative, artistic soul.

4. The **Number 4** in numerology represents stability and dependability. Like the earth beneath your feet, the number 4 is strong, sure, and true—a number you can always count on.

5. The **Number 5** in numerology represents freedom and adventure. A pro at change, 5 is highly adaptable and able to go with the flow. Number 5 is never one to stagnate, preferring to move on to the next great thing.

6. The **Number 6** in numerology represents unconditional love, symbolizing the heart. The love of the number 6 is a powerful force for healing and nurturing.

7. The **Number 7** in numerology represents digging deeper. It is, spiritually, a very special number as it aligns with the seven planets, the seven days of the week, and seven notes of music on the musical scale. The 7 is a very wise and spiritual number, but it leads with its head, not its heart.

8. The **Number 8** in numerology represents achievement and success. Some followers of numerology have even changed

their names in order to get more number 8's in their numerology charts!

9. The **Number 9** in numerology has the energy of completion; in contrast to its counterpart number 1 (the beginning), number 9 represents the end. It is not a final end that 9 represents, but rather the end of one journey and the possibilities of the next!

There are three special double-digit numbers that numerologists do not break down into their Root Numbers by summing the two digits. These special numbers are called **Master Numbers**. A brief explanation of the meaning of each is below.

- The **Master Number 11** in numerology is the most spiritual of numbers, representing dreamers and visionaries. The number 11 represents the human potential to reach spiritual enlightenment!

- The **Master Number 22** is said to be the master builder. This number represents practical idealism and the progress of humankind as a whole.

- The **Master Number 33** is the rarest of Master Numbers in a numerology chart. This number represents the master teacher, destined to share the enlightenment of the Master Number 33 with the world.

Each letter of the alphabet is then said to correspond to a number 1-9:

1. A, J, S
2. B, K, T
3. C, L, U

4. D, M, V
5. E, N, W
6. F, O, X
7. G, P, Y
8. H, Q, Z
9. I, R

The basic practice of numerology is then to convert each individual letter that makes up a word into its corresponding number. Those numbers are then summed, or added, together. If the sum total is a two-digit number or higher (unless the number is 11, 22, or 33), the individual digits are summed again until you are left with a number 1-9—the Root Number.

The numbers 11, 22, and 33 are considered Master Numbers, and they do not get broken down into their Root Numbers in numerological calculations. This is because the three Master Numbers have special attributes and together make up what numerologists call the Triangle of Enlightenment.

This may sound complicated, but it's actually quite simple! Let's put all you have learned together and take a look at a couple of examples. For instance, the name Katherine:

K = 2, A = 1, T = 2, H = 8, E = 5, R = 9, I = 9, N = 5, E = 5

So:

K+A+T+H+E+R+I+N+E = 2+1+2+8+5+9+9+5+5 = 46 = 4+6 = 10 = 1+0 = 1

The single digit number that ultimately corresponds to the name Katherine is 1.

However, to fully understand what numerology has to say about you as a person, you will need to calculate numbers for much more than just your first name. We will go into a great deal more depth about the various numbers you can calculate for yourself, and why you should calculate them, in the next section.

Let's look at another example. For instance, a date. Let's say, the year 2020:

2 + 0 + 2 + 0 = 4

So, the single digit number that corresponds to 2020 is 4.

Power Numbers

Power Numbers are any double-digit numbers that are not 11, 22, or 33—that is, their individual digits do not appear in the Triangle of Enlightenment. Power Numbers like 44, 55, and so forth are not Master Numbers. But as their name implies, they are indeed powerful numbers.

The presence of duplicate digits intensifies the influence of these numbers and makes the energy attributes of each amplified. But there is another layer to these numbers, which is the single digit Root Number to which they sum. This Root Number influences the vibrational frequency of the Power Number, so that 88, for example, does not only connote the double energy of the 8s but also the energy of the 7 to which it ultimately sums. (8+8 = 16 = 1+6 = 7)

These Power Numbers should not appear in your Core Numbers within your numerological chart. If you did calculate a Power Number for one of your Core Numbers, you would simply sum the two digits to break it down to its Root Number. (For instance, 55 = 5+5 = 10 = 1+0 = 1)

Angel Numbers

What does it mean when you keep seeing the number 1111 everywhere? Numbers like 222, 1234, etc. are called Angel Numbers.

Angel numbers are similar to Master Numbers, but for one major difference: They do not show up in your numerology chart. When calculating a numerology chart, you will always break down Angel Numbers by summing their individual digits.

The magic of Angel Numbers instead is outside of your numerology chart, in your everyday life. These are the three, four (or more) digit repeating numbers that may seem to follow you everywhere: 11:11 on the clock, $11.11 at the checkout counter, and so on and so forth. Angel Numbers are believed to be divine guidance and a sign that you are on the right path. It is said that Angel Numbers are the way angels communicate with us.

In general, when you see repeating Angel Numbers popping up in your life, it is a sign that someone is watching and encouraging you.

Your Core Numbers

There are many different numbers and calculations that make up a complete numerological chart. The five most important numbers in your chart are called the Core Numbers. If you want to try out numerology for yourself, these are the numbers you should calculate for your own chart first. These Core Numbers include the Life Path Number, the Destiny or Expression Number, the Soul Urge Number, the Personality Number, and the Birth Day Number.

Your **Life Path Number** is an important numerological number that equates essentially to your sun sign in astrology; it is calculated using your full date of birth. To calculate your life path number, you will simply sum the digits in your day of birth, then sum the digits in your month of birth, then sum the digits in your year of birth, and break all of these down to single digit numbers. Then, sum these numbers together and break them down to a single digit one final time. For example:

April 1, 1994

April = 4

1 = 1

1994 = 1+9+9+4 = 23 = 2+3 = 5

4 + 1 + 5 = 10 = 1+0 = 1

So, a person who is born on April 1, 1994, has a life path number of 1, which means they are a natural leader.

Your **Destiny Number** is calculated using your full name, including first name, middle name (if you have one), and last name. Traditionally, birth names are used—but some numerologists believe that you can in fact change your Destiny Number by changing your name. To calculate your Destiny Number, you will use the numbers-to-letters chart in the previous section to convert the letters in your first, middle, and last names into numbers. Then, sum these numbers individually and reduce to a single digit. Finally, sum these single digits together and then reduce again if necessary. For example:

Mary Ann Rose

Mary = 4+1+9+7 = 21 = 2+1 = 3

Ann = 1+5+5 = 11 (Remember, we do not break 11 down into its Root Number because it is a Master Number!)

Rose = 9+6+1+5 = 21 = 2+1 = 3

3+11+3 = 17 = 1+7 = 8

So, an individual named Mary Ann Rose has a destiny number of 8.

Your **Soul Urge Number**, sometimes called, simply, your Soul Number, is said to reveal your heart's deepest desires. This number is calculated using only the vowels in your name, because vowels are said to represent the inner self.

Be sure to only count any Y's in your name (for your calculation) if those Y's are used as vowels, not as consonants. For example:

Charles Liam Yancy

Charles = A+E = 1+5 = 6

Liam = I+A = 9+1 = 10 = 1+0 = 1

Yancy = A+Y = 1+7 = 8

6+1+8 = 15 = 1+5 = 6

So, Charles Liam Yancy has a Soul Urge Number of 6.

Your **Personality Number** represents who you are on the outside. Like vowels are said to show the inner self, consonants show the outer self. To calculate your Personality Number, use only the consonants in your name. To take Charles Liam Yancy as an example again:

Charles = C+H+R+L+S = 3+8+9+3+1 = 24 = 2+4 = 6

Liam = L+M = 3+4 = 7

Yancy = Y+N+C = 7+5+3 = 15 = 1+5 = 6

6+7+6 = 19 = 1+9 = 10 = 1+0 = 1

So, Charles's Personality Number is 1, very different from his Soul Urge Number.

The last of the Core Numbers is called the **Birth Day Number**, and it does not require a calculation: Instead, you simply examine the day of the month on which you're born. So, if you were born on April 4th, your Birth Day Number is 4, and if you were born on November 28th, your Birth Day Number is 28. Your Birth Day Number represents your unique gifts to the world and is one of the few times in numerology when double-digit numbers are examined.

Practicing Numerology Today

As you learned in this chapter, numerological calculations are actually quite simple and easy to understand! They are calculations you can do yourself, if you are patient, though many free and paid online calculators are available to do the work for you. If you are interested in learning more about numerology, I have an entire book available on Amazon that is dedicated solely to the topic. You can also seek the aid of a professional numerologist if you would like to have your numerology chart done by a master!

Once you know the numbers in your numerology chart, you can use them to better understand your potential in life and make sure you reach it. Numerology, like astrology, is also useful for determining compatibility in relationships, so you may want to calculate your partner, or crush's, life path number, too!

Chapter Eight: Tasseography

Tasseography, also called tasseomancy, is commonly known as tea leaf reading. However, this means of divination does not actually require tea leaves at all; tasseography can be practiced by reading coffee grounds, wine sediments, or any other detritus left in the bottom of a cup or glass that has been drunk. *Tasse*, in fact, actually comes from the French word meaning cup.

Tasseography is an interpretive form of divination that involves the recognition of symbols and imagery in the tea leaves (or other detritus) at the bottom of the cup. This makes tea leaf reading one of the most accessible forms of divination to the average person, as it requires no special occult tools or magical instruments—just your favorite tea and a cup! Despite being so easy to use, tasseography is not one of the more popular forms of divination used today in the west, and as a result, it is often misunderstood.

The History of Tasseography

When you think of tea leaf reading, you may think of ancient China, but this is a common misconception. While tea may have originated in China, there is actually no evidence that the ancient Chinese practiced tasseography! This rumor might have begun as a way to lend legitimacy and exoticness to the practice by its actual founders: 17th century Europeans.

Tea first made its way to Europe by trade in the 17th century. At first, it was mostly a delicacy only for the wealthy and noble, but over time tea became more commonly enjoyed by everyone, regardless of class or status. There were no tea bags back then, so finding sediment of tea leaves in the bottom of your otherwise empty cup was standard. We do not know who first began the practice of divining from these leaves, although there is evidence that tea leaf reading evolved from earlier practices of reading coffee or wine sediments.

As tea consumption became more common throughout Europe, the practice of divining through tasseography did as well. Thus, tea leaf reading became wildly popular throughout Victorian England until it fell out of favor in the early 20th century due to the invention of the teabag.

Symbols in the Tea Leaves

Tasseographers have observed and made note of consistent patterns and configurations found in the tea leaves as well as their common interpretations over the generations. One such source of these interpretations is a book written by someone who called themselves only 'A Highland Seer'. This book, called *Tea-Cup Reading and Fortune-Telling by Tea Leaves*, was written in 1881 and is available to read for free on the internet today.

This book contains over 150 individual symbols and their interpretations. For the sake of brevity, in this book, we will cover the most common categories of symbols and few popular examples. The most common symbols can be divided into five categories: **animals**, **mythical beings**, **objects**, **letters**, and **numbers**. The meanings of letters and numbers are somewhat self-explanatory, though you as the diviner must use your own intuition to make sense of this communication.

Some common animals to be seen in the tea leaves include:

- Bird: luck, fortune, good news
- Cat: difficulties caused by treachery
- Elephant: good health

- Monkey: deceit in love
- Owl: a warning omen of sickness or poverty
- Swan: good luck and happy marriage

The category of mythical beings includes:

- Angel: good news, good fortune in love
- Dragon: big, sudden change
- Mermaid: misfortune
- Unicorn: scandal

Some common objects to be seen in the tea leaves include:

- Anchor: luck, success in business or love
- Axe: difficulties overcome
- Boat: a visiting friend
- Coffin: long illness or death of a loved one
- Harp: marriage, success in love
- Knife: a warning of disaster
- Pine tree: continuous happiness
- Wheel: a coming inheritance

The Importance of the Cup

When reading tea leaves, the placement of the teacup on the surface of the table is very important, as is the location of the tea leaves and symbols relative to the cup. As the *tasseo* in tasseomancy tells us, it is all about the cup from which you read!

The teacup handle is of utmost importance. The handle of the cup represents the energy conduit connecting the diviner and querent here in the earthly realm to the psychic realm. It also symbolizes the querent and must be placed facing the direction of south, symbolizing the querent's current state. Tea leaves found near the handle of the cup tell the diviner about events relating to the querent's inner situation, while leaves found directly across from the handle (facing north) are all about outside influences.

For the purpose of interpretation, the teacup can be divided into three distinct segments: the **rim**, the **sides**, and the **bottom** of the cup. The rim of the cup symbolizes the present, the sides of the cup symbolize the near future, and the bottom of the cup represents the distant future. So, you can interpret not just the shapes you see but also their relative position as a place in time in the querent's life.

You can even purchase special cups designed for the practice of tasseography! These cups come "divided" with painted lines on the inside so that you can see the various quadrants of the cup while you are reading. These are often connected with astrology and mimic astrological houses.

Practicing Tasseography Today

As explained in this chapter, tea leaf reading is a particularly accessible form of divination. All you need to get started is some loose leaf tea and a cup and saucer.

If you are not familiar with loose leaf tea, be aware that the emptied contents of a tea bag will not do for purposes of tasseography, because these leaves are ground up too finely to produce the symbols you will interpret in the cup. It is essential that you use loose leaf tea. Beginners are recommended to use specifically loose leaf black tea, which should be easy to find at a grocery store.

When you are ready to begin, place your tea leaves directly in the cup without the use of any type of strainer or infuser. Pour hot water (preferably from a kettle, not the microwave--but whatever you have will do) over the leaves. Because you will leave the leaves in the cup, there is no need for steeping. Simply wait for the tea to cool to a drinkable temperature before taking a sip. You can use this time to focus on your query.

Continue to contemplate your question or issue while you enjoy a cup of hot tea. When there is only about a tablespoon of liquid remaining in the teacup, swirl the cup in your hand three times. Next, carefully turn the teacup over and place it upside down on the saucer, so that the little remaining liquid runs out. Leave the cup upside down on the saucer for a moment or two, then turn it around in three complete rotations.

Finally, turn the cup back right-side up on the saucer and position it so that the handle is facing the south. You are ready to read your tea leaves!

You can use the guide to symbols above as a starting point. The internet is a great, free resource for more information about any of the symbols you may see. But your intuition is the greatest resource of all, so pay close attention to what feelings and sensations the symbols in your tea leaves connote for you. Your own personal meaning is more accurate than any interpretation found in a book.

Final Words

As you have learned, anyone can practice divination, regardless of their birth right or natural clairvoyant powers: It simply takes a combination of learning interpretive symbols and flexing your intuitive muscles. Knowing this is a powerful tool. We have pulled back the shroud that obscures the practice of divination and relegates it to the unknown. Instead, the power to seek answers from the void is in your own hands.

You are set up now with a basic knowledge of the most popular modern forms of divination today, and if you have been following along, you now know how to practice astrology, tarot cards, runes, pendulum dowsing, scrying, numerology, and tea leaf reading! This is an impressive repertoire of divination skills. If you continue to practice, and read books to learn more, you will surely become a master diviner in time.

www.ingramcontent.com/pod-product-compliance
Lightning Source LLC
LaVergne TN
LVHW021737060526
838200LV00052B/3330